by Jillian Powell

HODDER
Wayland

an imprint of Hodder Children's Books

Titles in the series

Summer on the farm
Autumn on the farm
Winter on the farm
Spring on the farm

Picture Acknowledgements
The publishers would like to thank the following for allowing their photographs to be reproduced in this book: Agripicture: Peter Dean 19; Cephas Picture Library *title page* (Mick Rock), 7 top (Lance Smith), 12, 13 top (Frank B. Higham), 13 bottom (Nigel Blythe) 17 (Frank B Higham); Bruce Coleman Ltd 14 (Graham Jennings), 15 bottom, 16 bottom (Gordon Langsbury), 18 (Julie Fryer); Eye Ubiquitous 5 bottom (David Nunn); Farmers Weekly Picture Library 10 top, 19; Frank Lane Picture Agency 5 top (Ray F. Bird), 6 (D Dugan), 7 bottom (Silvestris), 9 (Peter Dean), 23 top (R.P. Lawrence), 27 top (P Reynolds), 27 bottom (D.T. Grewcock); The Hutchison Library 26 (Jeremy Hall); Natural History Photographic Agency 4 (G I Bernard), 10 bottom (Patrick Fagot), 12 (Brian Hawkes), 15 top (David Tomlinson), 16 top (Roger Tidman), 20 (David Woodfall), 22 (Manfred Danegger),23 bottom (David Tomlinson), 24 (William Paton), 25 top (E.A. Janes), 25 bottom (G I Bernard); Oxford Scientific Films Ltd 8 (G.A. Maclean), 15 top (Harold Taylor), 16 bottom (Tony Tilford), 17 (David Cayless); Tony Stone Worldwide *front cover* (Hugh Sitton), *back cover* (David Austen); Survival Anglia 11 top (Ton Nyssen); Wayland Picture Library 11 bottom, 16 top, 21 (both), 28, 29, 30 (both), 31 (both).

Series editor: Francesca Motisi
Book editor: Joan Walters
Series and book designer: Jean Wheeler

First published in Great Britain in 1996
by Wayland (Publishers) Ltd
This edition printed in 2001 by Hodder Wayland,
an imprint of Hodder Children's Books

© Hodder Wayland 1996

British Cataloguing in Publication Data
Powell, Jillian
Autumn on the farm. - (The farming year)
1. Agriculture - Juvenile literature 2. Autumn - Juvenile literature
I. Title II. Series
630

ISBN 0-7502-3420-2

Typeset by Jean Wheeler
Printed and bound in Hong Kong

Contents

Introduction

Autumn is a season of changes.
Every day the sun rises a little later
and sets a little earlier, so the days
begin to get shorter.

Some days are warm and sunny.
Other days bring wind and rain.
At night it may be cold enough
for frost.

Heavy rain, wind and frost can spoil crops. The farmer must harvest and store the crops before the bad weather comes.

The farmer must also make sure there is plenty of food for the farm animals during the cold autumn and winter months, when the grass stops growing. Hay is stored for winter feed.

Harvesting root crops

By the autumn, potatoes and sugar beet have grown big enough to harvest. These are called root crops because we eat the roots of the plants.

The farmer uses a special machine called a root crop harvester. It lifts the plants out of the ground and shakes the earth off them.

The vegetables fall into a trailer and are taken back to the farm. The potatoes will be sold in supermarkets and other shops.

Sugar beet (right) will be taken to factories where machines take the sugar from the roots.

Harvesting the maize crop

Maize is ripe and ready to harvest in the autumn. It is grown for people and animals to eat. There are different types of maize. We eat it as cornflakes and popcorn.

Sweetcorn is a crop which is very like maize. Here, sweetcorn cobs are being harvested.

Another type of maize is made into a food called silage, to feed to animals during the winter months.

The farmer harvests maize for silage using a machine called a forage harvester. It cuts the plants and then chops up the leaves, stems and cobs into small pieces. It is taken back to the farmyard in a trailer to be stored.

The fruit harvest

Sunshine helps the fruit trees make sugar in the fruits, so they become sweet and ripe.

Fruits like apples (right), pears and plums (below) are ready to be picked in the autumn.

We can tell when a fruit is ripe because it changes colour.

Fruit has to be picked carefully. Some fruit farms have special fruit-picking machines which gently knock the fruit off the trees.

On small farms, farm workers pick the fruit by hand. The fruit is carried back to the farm in a trailer.

The fruit is sorted into sizes and stored in big trays. Any fruit which is not perfect is taken out and sent off to be made into fruit juice.

All the good fruit is stored in cold, dry sheds. This is so it will not go bad before it is taken by lorry to fruit and vegetable markets.

Harvesting hops

Hops are climbing plants which grow along posts and wires. The flowers from hops are used to give beer its special bitter taste and to help it keep longer.

At harvest time, the farmer cuts the strings holding the hop plants so that they fall into a trailer.

The hops are taken to a harvesting machine which picks the hops away from the stems and leaves.

The hops are taken to a special building called an oast house, where they are stored and left to dry.

Autumn ploughing

As soon as the harvest is over, the farmer starts thinking about the next crop. The first job is to prepare the fields using a tractor pulling a plough. This turns over the earth and buries all the stubbly straw left after the harvest. The straw stubble and weeds rot back into the earth and make more food for next year's crops.

The farmer then fixes a tool called a harrow to the tractor. A harrow has big teeth to break up the earth and make it ready for sowing new seeds.

Sometimes the farmer spreads animal manure over the fields before ploughing. It is full of goodness and food for plants.

Now the fields are ready for the farmer to sow wheat, barley or oats for harvest next summer.

Cutting hedges

Hedges grow between fields of different crops. They also stop farm animals from getting out of the fields.

Hedges give shade and shelter to animals all year, and protect crops from wind, rain and snow.

Hedges also provide a home for wild animals, birds and insects.

If the farmer waits until late autumn before cutting the hedges, there will be hedgerow fruits and seeds which birds and animals can eat.

This tractor carries a hedge cutter which has strong metal teeth to cut back the branches. Cutting hedges helps them grow thick and strong.

Making silage

In autumn the farmer must plan ahead so that the farm animals will have plenty to eat when there is no fresh grass. The grass will stop growing as the days get shorter and the weather gets colder.

The farmer cuts the grass to make a food for the winter called silage. The grass is cut and sucked up by a machine called a forage harvester.

The grass is gathered and wrapped tightly in black plastic so no light or air can get in. This keeps it soft and juicy. Some big farms have tall buildings for making silage called silos. You may see silage stored on a farm under black plastic with old car tyres on top.

Beef and dairy farming

Farmers who farm cattle for milk or beef keep
their animals outdoors as long as possible in
the autumn. The cattle feed on grass growing
in the fields. This is called grazing.

As the autumn weather gets colder, the farmer may bring the animals into covered yards where they stay warm and dry for the winter months.

They are given straw to sleep on, and they are fed with grass which has been made into hay or silage.

Some calves are born in the autumn. On dairy farms they feed on their mother's milk for the first few days. Then they are fed on dried milk by the farmer. The cow can then be milked twice a day in the milking parlour.

Deer farming

Autumn is the time of year called 'the rut' when female deer, called hinds, are mated with the male deer, called stags. The stags make a roaring noise and become very excited.

The hinds are put in groups with a stag for mating.
Deer calves are born the following spring.

By autumn the calves no longer need
their mother's milk. The farmer takes
them indoors, checks that they are
healthy and weighs them. Then they
are let out to graze on their own.

They will stay outdoors until the
weather turns cold and wet.

The sheep farm

In the autumn, female sheep, called ewes, are ready to mate with the rams. The farmer checks to see that the ewes and the rams are healthy before they are put together to mate.

The farmer knows when the sheep have mated because a coloured crayon tied to the ram leaves a mark on the ewe. The ewes will give birth to their lambs in the spring.

In autumn, sheep must be dipped in a bath with special chemicals in the water. This will kill any insects living in the sheep's wool. The sheep are sent through the dip one at a time.

The fish farm

As the autumn brings chilly weather, the water on the fish farm becomes colder. Fish swim in the deeper water, which is the warmest part. In cold water they grow more slowly and need less food.

The fish farmer gives them fish meal, which contains everything they need to keep healthy. Fish swim to the surface of the water to feed.

This Scottish fish farmer is harvesting large salmon, which he will sell.

The harvest festival

Autumn is the time when farmers finish harvesting the crops which have been growing through the spring and summer months.

Harvest festivals are held in schools and churches, to give thanks for all the cereal crops, fruit and vegetables which have ripened ready for harvest.

People bring fruit and vegetables which
have been growing in their gardens.
Sometimes there is a sheaf of wheat, or a
special sheaf-shaped loaf of bread.

On the farm, everyone is happy when the
harvest is safely gathered in.

The farming year calendar

Spring

Sowing crops for summer and autumn harvest

Harvesting vegetables grown through the winter

Fertilising and spraying crops against weeds and diseases

Lambing

Putting animals out to graze

Silage making

Summer

Harvesting vegetables and soft fruits

Watering crops

Haymaking

Silage making

Sheep shearing and sheep dipping

Harvesting crops such as wheat and barley

Autumn

Ploughing fields after
  harvest
Sowing winter wheat
  and barley
Harvesting fruits such as
  apples and pears
Harvesting potatoes and
  sugar beet
Autumn calving
Hedge trimming

Winter

Clearing and draining
  ditches
Pruning fruit trees
Housing animals
Early indoor lambing
Fertilising crops
Repairing farm
  buildings, fences
  and machinery

Glossary

Hay Grass that has been dried in the sun. It is used to feed farm animals in the winter.

Manure Animal waste, such as cow pats, mixed into the earth to help plants grow.

Mate When a male and female animal join together to produce babies.

Rams Male sheep.

Sheaf Cut wheat, tied up in a bundle.

Silage Grass or other crops harvested when green and kept juicy. It is fed to farm animals in winter.

Straw The stalks of grain crops, such as wheat, barley and oats.

Books to read

Farming Sue Hadden (Wayland, 1991)
Farming Ruth Thomson (Franklin Watts, 1994)
Let's Visit a Farm series S. Doughty & D. Bentley (Wayland, 1989-90)

Index